Then and Now

Life at Home

Vicki Yates

Heinemann
LIBRARY

www.heinemann.co.uk/library
Visit our website to find out more information about Heinemann Library books.

To order:
☎ Phone 44 (0) 1865 888066
🗎 Send a fax to 44 (0) 1865 314091
💻 Visit the Heinemann Bookshop at www.heinemann.co.uk/library to browse our catalogue and order online.

First published in Great Britain by Heinemann Library, Halley Court, Jordan Hill, Oxford OX2 8EJ, part of Pearson Education. Heinemann is a registered trademark of Pearson Education Ltd.

© Pearson Education Ltd 2008
First published in paperback in 2009
The moral right of the proprietor has been asserted.

Editorial: Charlotte Guillain and Vicki Yates
Design: Victoria Bevan, Joanna Hinton-Malivoire and Q2A solutions
Picture research: Ruth Blair and Q2A solutions
Production: Duncan Gilbert

Printed and bound in China by South China Printing Co. Ltd.

ISBN 978 0431 19186 7 (Hardback)
ISBN 978 0431 19194 2 (Paperback)

13 12 11 10 09
10 9 8 7 6 5 4 3 2 1

British Library Cataloguing in Publication Data
Yates, Vicki
Life at home. - (Then and now)
1. Home - Juvenile literature 2. Family - Juvenile literature 3. Social history - Juvenile literature
640
A full catalogue record for this book is available from the British Library.

Acknowledgements
The publishers would like to thank the following for permission to reproduce photographs: AKG-Images pp. **6**, **23**; Corbis pp. **9** (Steve Chenn), **21** (Randy Faris); Flickr p. **7** (Sarah Beth Photography); Istockphoto p. **18**; Library of Congress p. **16**; Photolibrary.com pp. **4**, **11**(Foodpix), **5** (Michael Hall/Photonica Inc), **8**, **20** (Vintage Images/Nonstock Inc), **13** (Johner Bildbyra), **15** (Fermariello Mauro/Science Photo Library), **17** (Frank P Wartenberg/Picture Press), **19** (Charles Gullung/Photonica Inc); Rex Features p. **14**; Science & Society p. **10** (Royal Photographic Society); Shutterstock p. **22** (Lance Bellers); USDA pp. **12**, **23**; Vintage Images p. **23** (Nonstock Inc/Photolibrary)

Cover photograph of girl in tin bath reproduced with permission of Rex Features and photograph of girl in bath reproduced with permission of Corbis (Cameron). Back cover photograph of mangle reproduced with permission of Shutterstock (Lance Bellers)

Every effort has been made to contact copyright holders of any material reproduced in this book. Any omissions will be rectified in subsequent printings if notice is given to the publishers.

Contents

What is a home?

A home is where people live.

A home is where people sleep, eat, and play.

Long ago people lived in caves.

Today we live in buildings.

Keeping warm

Long ago all homes had a fireplace.
Fires kept people warm.

Today most homes have heating.
Some homes still have fireplaces.

Food and drink

Long ago people cooked over a fire.

Today people use a cooker.

Long ago people got water from a well.

Today people get water from
a tap.

Keeping clean

Long ago there were no bathrooms.
People washed in a tin bath.

Today homes have a bathroom
with hot and cold water.

Long ago people washed all their clothes by hand.

Today people use a washing machine.

Light

Long ago people used candles for light.

Today we have electric lights.

Let's compare

Long ago life at home was very different.

Which is better? Then or now?

What is it?

Long ago this object was used at home. Do you know what it is?

22

Answer on p. 24

Picture glossary

 **cave** big hole in the side of a hill or cliff

 **fireplace** somewhere to light a fire

 **well** deep hole with water at the bottom

Index

Answer to question on p. 22: This is a mangle. People used it to squeeze water from wet clothes.

Note to Parents and Teachers
Before reading
Tell the children how homes have changed since you were a child. Encourage them to ask you questions. If possible, ask an elderly person to come and talk to the children about their home when they were young.

After reading
• Tell the children they are going to act what it was like in homes a long time ago. Remind them that the only heating was fires downstairs so it was cold when they got up in the morning. Remind them about cooking on the fire. Explain that it is Monday and everyone had to do washing. Where will they go to get the water? How will they wash the clothes? What will they use for lights when it gets dark? What will they use for a bath?
• Sing to the tune of "Here we go round the mulberry bush" a "Then and Now" version. For example: "Then we went round the mulberry bush etc/This is the way we dressed for school/washed our clothes/had a bath etc." Then switch to a modern version: "Now we go round the mulberry bush..." and change the words to a modern experience.